Your Big Story

For my Hannah Bear, who has always loved a good story.

Text copyright © 2013 Andy Liples
Illustrations copyright © 2013 Ruth Cottingham

Published by Morning Joy Media.

Visit www.morningjoymedia.com for more information on bulk discounts and special promotions, or e-mail your questions to info@morningjoymedia.com.

The text of this book is set in Chaparral Pro and Gill Sans Ultra Bold Condensed.
The illustrations are done with pencil and watercolor on watercolor paper, with fabric accents.

Publisher's Cataloging in Publication data

Liples, Andy.
     Your Big Story / written by Andy Liples ; illustrated by Ruth Cottingham
          p. cm.
     Summary: A child learns she is part of a big story that began with God before the creation of the world.
     ISBN 978-1-937107-17-8 (pbk.)
     1. Christian life—Juvenile literature. 2. God—Biblical teaching—Juvenile literature. I. Cottingham, Ruth, ill. II. Title.

Printed in the United States of America

Your Big Story

by

Andy Liples

Illustrated by

Ruth Cottingham

Morning Joy Media

Spring City, Pennsylvania

I know how much you love to hear a good story, but did you know that you are in your very own story? It's actually part of a bigger story—a big, BIG story that started a long, LONG, LOOONG time ago.

Your story started before there were people or puppies, beetles or butterflies, trees or rivers, or even the stars. It started when there was only GOD, but God decided that this just wouldn't do.

So God created the STARS. He created the rivers and trees. He created beetles and butterflies. He created puppies.

God thought all of this was good, but it still wasn't enough, and that's where we come in.

God decided to create people. So He made a man named Adam and a woman named Eve. Every day, God would meet with Adam and Eve and walk with them through a beautiful garden called Eden.

Of all the things God created, people were His favorite, and they still are, because He made them like He is—able to think and feel and love.

Adam and Eve eventually had babies who grew up to be adults and have babies of their own. Those babies grew up to be adults and have babies too. This pattern has repeated for thousands of years and has continued today—all the way to you. You are one of God's favorite creations because you were created to be like Him.

God loves all of the people He has created, but not all of them have done good things. There was a time long ago in your story when most of the people of the world only thought about themselves and didn't listen to what God wanted them to do.

But a man named Noah listened to God and obeyed Him.

When a big flood destroyed the rest of the world, God kept Noah, his family, and all kinds of animals safe on a giant boat called an ark. God still keeps us safe today, and he's very happy when we listen to Him and obey what he says.

As the world filled with more and more people, God loved each one. He knew we were going to need help knowing how to obey Him and do the right things. So He spoke to a man named Moses about ten special rules called the Ten Commandments that teach us how to love God and how to love others. Here's what they are:

1 Always put God first

2 Worship God only

3 Don't misuse God's Name

4 Keep one day a week to rest

5 Obey your Mom and Dad

6 Don't kill other people

7 Stay true to your husband or wife

8 Don't steal

9 Don't lie

10 Don't be jealous of other people

These rules were not just for the people back then. They are for you and me now, and when we follow them we make God very happy.

As God's people, we tried our best to live by His special rules, but we kept making mistakes. That didn't stop God from wanting to show us how we should live though, and He still missed walking side by side with people as He did with Adam and Eve in the garden.

So He decided to do something very **SPECIAL**. He sent His son, **JESUS**, to earth to live with the people He created. Jesus did not come to earth in an airplane or a rocket ship. He came the same way you did—as a little baby. Jesus had to learn to walk just like you did. He learned to talk just like you did.

And just like we celebrate your birthday every year, we get
to celebrate Jesus' birthday every year too, at Christmas.

When Jesus grew up, He spent his time teaching people about God and healing people who were sick or hurt. He loved all the people He saw, and He especially loved children. Once when little children came to see Jesus, his friends tried to stop them because those friends thought Jesus was too busy.

But Jesus told them to let the children come and see Him. You see, Jesus has always loved children, and He's never too busy when we need Him.

Even though Jesus loved all of the people that He got to see while He was on earth, there were still some who didn't love Him or do what God wanted. Jesus knew there had to be a punishment for disobeying God, but because He loved people so much He decided to take their punishment for them.

Even though Jesus didn't do anything wrong, He was punished by being put on a cross to die.

We still do bad things sometimes, but God can forgive us because Jesus has already taken the punishment for those bad things.

As you learn and grow, sometimes you'll need to be punished too. But God will always forgive you if you ask Him because on that day, Jesus took the biggest punishment of all for you.

As you can imagine, Jesus' friends were very sad when Jesus died on the cross, but I'm happy to say that the story didn't end there. After Jesus was in the grave for three days, He came back to life. Jesus' friends were so excited to see Him again!

Jesus was glad that His friends believed in Him, but before He went back to heaven, He said that someday people would be blessed for believing without seeing Him.

Now, you are one of those people. You believe in Jesus even though you haven't seen Him.

And that brings us to one of my favorite characters in this big story—YOU!

We were so happy the day that you were born. We had waited months to finally meet you. We did everything we could to prepare for you—buying your clothes, setting up your room, and picking out your name.

As excited as we were for you to be born, God was even more excited—and He had done even more to prepare for you. After all, He created the whole world you live in, and He has been with your family through floods and all sorts of adventures to get them here to you.

Isn't that exciting? You were created by the One who made everything, and you are one of His favorite parts. He has given you rules to help you do the right things, but He is always willing to forgive you when you make mistakes.

He loves you and is never too busy to hear from you.
He just asks that you believe in Him, and someday
you'll walk side by side with Him in heaven.

So now with years ahead of you, you get to write the rest of **YOUR BIG STORY**. Just promise me that when you do, you will remember how you fit into this big, wonderful story that started so long ago.

ANDY LIPLES lives in Skippack, Pennsylvania, with his wife, Jessica, their two kids, Tommy and Hannah, and a curious puppy named Cody. *Your Big Story* is Andy's first trek into the world of authoring, and it has been a blast. He hopes you enjoy reading this book as much he enjoyed writing it, and most of all—he hopes you are blessed to realize that you are a part of something amazing.

RUTH COTTINGHAM and her husband, Jim, are both art teachers. They have seven children, and a little ten-year-old girl, Desiree, who now is also part of their family. Some of their children are older and grown, and have children of their own. Ruth and Jim live in New Jersey with their family and their new puppy, Flomar.

CPSIA information can be obtained
at www.ICGtesting.com
Printed in the USA
LVIC081223100313
323544LV00010B

* 9 7 8 1 9 3 7 1 0 7 1 7 8 *